I0474436

RECESSION PROOF BILLIONAIRE

FINANCIAL FLAK JACKET

AND FLIGHT PLAN FOR TOMORROW'S BILLIONAIRE

Dr. R. A. Benson

This publication is designed to provide
authoritative information regarding the
subject matter covered. It is published
with the understanding that the
publisher is not engaging in rendering
legal, accounting or other professional
service. If professional assistance is
required, it should be sought.

ISBN: 978-0-557-88036-2

Printed in the United States of America

TABLE OF CONTENTS

CHAPTER

1

What's A Tomorrow's Billionaire?

A million dollars just isn't what it used to be... In this day and time, the thoughts of being a millionaire are still just as wonderful as in times past, but the value of life that million dollars can afford you in today's economy just isn't the stuff that legacies are made of. Let's face it, once you buy the his and her autos, house, college tuition for the offspring, and the like, you are back to budgeting and economizing to maintain what little "wealth" you still have. This is the harsh reality, realized by so many athletes, and celebrities these days. In these changing times, it would appear that on the average, today's millionaire, is tomorrow's used-to-be millionaire, if diversification is not sought. Millionaires rarely become wealthy from doing just one thing. That is the number one rule, of being a mogul, tycoon, or king of your own sovereign nation.

This book however, is about being a billionaire, but not only that, it is about being a Recession-Proof Billionaire ™. This text was written to inspire and initiate a movement of capitalism amongst the "common man", and create an air of sovereignty and international citizenship, that will spread to the outermost shores of this world that, we are autonomous inhabitants of.

In a time where the poor man is already poor, and the rich man has convinced the poor man, that he will somehow become poorer since the rich man has become poorer, due to a downturn in proposed profits, you must see through the propaganda. This is foolishness, and you must not allow this wicked lie to contaminate your potentially successful future. The only way to survive the flood is to build an ark. Place yourself in the winning position, for if you are on the bottom, what do you really have to loose, by dedicating 100% of yourself to reach for success.

There are three questions, that those lacking wealth must ask themselves:

1. What genetically separates you from any billionaire that exists on Earth?
2. Why are they so special, that God has blessed them with great wealth?
3. Why can't you ever obtain the wealth, that you so desire?

The answers to these three questions are:

1. Nothing.
2. They are not, and he hasn't, really.
3. You can, and More!!!

So many people take the, "Some guy's have all the luck" attitude, and resign to the notion of failure, before the opening bell has rung. It is no one's job, but yours' to assure that your goals and objectives are met. <u>Billionaires don't *dream*, for they are visionaries that *visualize* the realities, that they are destined to manifest.</u>

This book is written in a historic time of economic turmoil on a global scale, and those who did not have anything invested in the fallen regime need not worry, in fact, celebration is in order. Opportunity is everywhere, all over the world. This text will show you a different picture of the "global financial crisis" and a way to not only become wealthy in spite of, and by way of, this 'crisis', but also how to become a virtually invisible international tycoon, able to control billions of dollars, legally, and secretly. The thinking has to switch from victim to victor, in these times of mass deception. Be the one there to pick up the pieces, and there is more than just wealth, but also power that can rival that of political appointment, to the highest post.

Just as there is always a casket maker, undertaker, and florist to benefit from death, while others mourn; there are those that rise to great financial heights, while the financial powers of the world appear to be on their knees (notice I said "appear"). How is it possible to succeed when all signs point to potential failure in a time that is marred with low financial esteem? Be the change that the world is looking for, and wealth will automatically flow!

In This Book You Will Learn About:

- Starting a business and national franchising

- Political-style campaigning to gain community support

- Becoming a national business

- International Citizenship

- Expatriation

- Forming an International Business Corporation (IBC)

- Forming an International Nonprofit Organization
- Offshore companies, bank accounts, and trusts
- Buying and securing islands
- Creating Offshore Financial Institutions
- Supplying aid to small nations
- Securing large amounts of gold secretly
- Existing without the need for a Social Security Number
- Monopolization by competing with yourself
- Investing in power plants, refineries, airports, nautical fleets,

water processing facilities, to sustain your empire

- And much more...

This humble text is obviously not to operate as an absolute, end-all-be-all reference, for the size of this text does not allow for elaborate details about every procedure, however, enough information is offered to give the serious reader ample knowledge to do his own due diligence. The author believes that the journey to the post in life outlined within these pages, should be more like a scavenger hunt for knowledge, than an ABC course. There is no one-size-fits-all remedy for achieving the stature that this book defines, and it is a job that takes a lot of creativity, and an equal amount of research and study. The billionaire get-rich-quick scheme is truly non-existent, and anything that is worth obtaining, is worth working hard for. If you ever meet a billionaire that is lazy, his riches will more than likely be that of inheritance and not truly earned, by the sweat of his own brow. International capitalism is not a spectator sport. But, if you feel that you have what it takes to take the bull by the horns and create a legacy for your family that will outlive even your grandchildren, this book will operate as your billionaire planning toolkit, flight plan, and Financial Flak Jacket ™.

CHAPTER

2

In Times of Peace...

As the saying goes, "In times of peace... prepare for war." These words define the diligence of tomorrow's billionaires, and the innovation and intuition that these entrepreneurs possess, to realize that, it is always calmest just before the storm. Individuals with this insight operate as the problem solvers, and saviors in times of disaster. Those that provide remedy in times of peril, are rewarded with loyalty and additional wealth, and the bigger the disaster, the greater the wealth and loyalty gained, by the savior of the day.

This is the sole reason that banks have etched out such a strong threshold of power globally with no end in sight. They found ways to become, "too big to fail" so that even when they were on the ropes, the failure of the banks appeared to pose a direct threat to the "system", and let some tell it, life itself. He who designs a system possesses the ability to pull the plug on the system. If the system fails, do the controllers of the system go broke, and become indigent? Of course not, but everyone on the other side of the table, who depend on the system, are left to fend for themselves, in the barren wastelands left behind. But this is not the case for the almighty, Recession-Proof Billionaire™ (RPB), for this Financial Juggernaut™, scales the mountain, surveys the landscape, and plans for his strategic attack.

The RPB is defined by his ability to strategize and execute his plan of attack with willful intent. The main goal of the RPB is to remain mission-oriented in all actions and affairs. This chapter looks at the mission of establishing a financial empire in a warfare framework, because warfare is planning and execution at its highest degree, and that is what the RPB requires. If you remove warfare from the context of violence and casualties, you are left with the hallmarks of true success. Let's look at the non-violent fundamentals involved in warfare:

- Patriotism
- Training
- Courage
- Planning
- Attack

We will take a closer look at these elements and define their use in the agenda of the RPB:

Patriotism – Patriotism is defined as national pride/loyalty; however in the instance of the RPB's mission the pride/loyalty is to the pending empire of the RPB which includes an international network of prosperity and influence.

Training – Everyone is familiar with the concept of basic training for new recruits that are preparing for war. This includes a six week training period where young men/women are transformed from ordinary high school graduates into fierce fighting machines. In the realm of the RPB the basic training may be based on higher education, past professional experience, or self-study (personal research). The RPB must be firm in his knowledge and never "gun-shy" when in the heat of the strategy's execution.

Courage – Courage often comes with the confidence one gains from the training period and the comfort and ease at which the soldier/RPB is able to perform the tasks necessary to accomplish the mission at hand.

Planning – The development of an effective strategy is one of the most important facets of warfare. The knowledge of where, when, and how the strike is going to occur is gained during this stage.

Attack – Once the troops are readied and the strategy is in place, the attack is staged and executed with surgical precision with little or no margin for error. The fact that lives are at stake never waivers form the mind of the troops or the General. In the case of the RPB the life that is at stake is the life that RPB is destined to live once the mission is accomplished.

When engaging in battle there is always an antagonist or enemy on the battlefield, to "go to war with". For the RPB the opposing force is a threefold monster that we refer to as the three F's. These being: Fear, Failure, and Falsehood. The RPB seeks to destroy the Fear of failure (or even success for that matter), the concept of Failure, and lastly all Falsehoods or untruths that are standing in the way of the RPB's success, are destroyed.

The theme of warfare strategizing and execution will be reoccurring in this text, and we begin with the War Room concept. This involves turning your office space into a convertible War Room. This is were the strategy will coagulate, and operates as the command center. The conversion of the office to a war room need not be a cosmetic or even physical one, but rather one of the mind. Put your proverbial General's Hat on when you enter this room, and that means basically making every decision with the sincerity, caution, and cunning of a General at war.

With the concept of the War Room being one of the mind, this allows for the Roving War Room™ concept (aka "Attache Command Center") to enter into the picture. This means every location serves as your makeshift command post when you are away from the office/official War Room.

CHAPTER

3

Coast to Coast

The RPB is not merely an entrepreneur, for this term does not fully describe the full dynamic of the RPB; for entrepreneurship is but only flight school for the ultra-ambitious Recession-Proof Billionaire™. While any entrepreneur can structure a business or three in a tight-knit area, or in a cluster of states as a means for success; the RPB is content only with viral growth of multiple operations, in a calculated effort to capture as much support and clientele as possible, and do so in as short of time period as possible. This takes meticulous planning and precise execution.

Business Fundamentals

Honestly, the fundamentals involved in starting a business are pretty standard all over the world. The structuring and management of a business in any country can be generally understood if the concept of structuring and operating a company in the U. S. is grasped. It is this reason that we will use the U. S. business structuring to outline how a typical business is established.

Corporate Structures – The various types

of corporate structures in the U. S. are: *Sole Proprietorship*—one party owns and operates; *Partnership*—two or more parties own and signify with Partnership Agreement; *Corporation*—stockholders own and board of directors operate; and *Limited Liability Company [LLC]*—'members' are legally liable only for their percentage of the company.

When establishing a business the legal documentation that is involved is similar from structure to structure. The Corporation is structured by filing a legal document called the Articles of Incorporation with the Secretary of State in most states. This document is called the Articles of Association when filing to establish an LLC. The "Articles" outline the company's location, mission, ownership information, and product/service information.

The deeper legal and taxation implications behind each structure should be evaluated before deciding what structure to utilize. The Author prefers the classic Corporation structure—the shareholding structure is favored over the recently-created and increasingly-popular LLC structure. The Small Business Administration's website has a business planner that has a section that details the structures and their legal/tax implications. Please seek this site for additional information on corporate structuring. It is important to gain a general sense of business before attempting to venture out on the journey outlined in this text. There are a wealth of details, that are too vast to mention here, that must be undertaken and considered while establishing and operating a business. Remember the importance of training from Chapter 2. Additionally, when seeking the steps required to initiate business in different lands, seek the World Bank Group's site called "Doing Business". This site features the steps needed to establish business in 183 economies worldwide.

Marketing – the RPB does not Market, so much as he "Campaigns" for business in a grassroots effort to attract clientele that resembles constituents more so than customers. This is accomplished by the use of "War Maps". War Maps are the RPB's equivalent of precinct/ward/region maps used by political campaigns. Locate maps of the area to be canvased—actual political precinct maps are ideal.

Political maps are divided into areas that are often indications of the demographic in certain areas. Demographic study is very important when establishing a presence in a new area. Find your target audience, and connect with this audience. If this target audience is defined by age group, sex, creed, etc., it may be best to also incorporate a "hotspot" canvas near colleges, office buildings, temples, churches, and other places that your demographic may be located.

To eliminate the possibility of ridicule never try to "sell" anything to people during canvasing operations. These outings are used as a means to "give" away coupons, product samples, and other promotional items that operate as "implants" or "agents" that will remind clients/customers that you are now there at their service.

The most important aspect of the canvasing operation is the brief verbal questionnaire that goes along with the offering. This questionnaire can be as few as two and no more than five questions, detailing the individual's preferences, frequency of use/visitation of like products/establishments, and so forth. There should be one question that sounds much like a political campaign question, to give the indication that the company is prepared to give back to the community it serves. This is often overlooked by failed businesses. Most successful businesses have some type of charitable effort or outreach in the communities they service. Companies do not however, use the methods outlined here for the RPB.

The compassionate and giving approach taken by a new company offers a personal feel that can not be matched with typical advertising. Knocking on doors and approaching people on the street is an all but lost marketing strategy. When you add the humanitarian/political twist to the equation you have the RPB groundwork.

The term "Coast to Coast" as defined by this chapter, relates to the strategic manipulation of the War Map. When looking to establish a nationwide campaign it is best to start on the coast —or boarders—of a nation. This makes it easier to establish export/import trade with nearby nations, and also contributes to the aura of national notoriety in a shorter period of time. When looking to create the massive wealth that is a billion dollars, the path of least resistance is always the proper route.

Once the coasts are established and thriving, a central location should be established in the "heart" of the nation. Once this is done, the expansion of locations from the central east and west will establish the growth of a nationally recognized and patronized establishment. Every major city is then to be targeted and the major radio, television, and printed ad (magazine /newspaper) campaign is initiated. After the coastal and central establishment is complete, the funding for the advertising campaign will be feasible, and well worth the return on investment. Even after the national campaign is launched, never move away from your grassroots foundation, that created your initial success.

The Coast to Coast method can be used to create national companies in any nation around the world. The structure is based on human psychology and it does not differ in any nation or region. Do not overlook the effectiveness of this strategy, because of its apparent simplicity. This is how politicians seek and obtain election.

While the transition of your office into a War Room need only be done in the mind, the addition of War Maps to the walls of the office at headquarters, complete with site-marking push pins makes for a marvelous visual and a morale booster as well.

Always look to "rally the troops" and give heart-felt "pep talks" to your associates and canvassers, to keep the team morale high. Offer random lunch and dinner incentives or even happy hour outings, when appropriate, to act as displays of appreciation to the surrounding cast helping to manifest your vision.

CHAPTER

4

Citizen Who?

Are you a citizen? If so a citizen of where? These questions when asked to the RPB will manifest answers different to 99% of the world. In fact the instant "knee-jerk" response that one makes to that statement will identify the readiness of that individual to set forth on the journey of the RPB. While when first heard it seems that this question may beg an obvious answer, the answer suitable for the RPB is rarely given.

Citizenship can be classified on various degrees, namely:

- **Municipal Citizenship** – this describes the city or township one identifies with

- **State Citizenship** – identification with the state one is living in

- **National Citizenship** – the most widely identified form of citizenship

- **World Citizenship** – this is the most powerful citizenship identification degree—contains no boundaries or boarders

The World Citizen realizes that it is feasible to go to France for French Fries, China for Chinese Food, and Italy for a

"Pizza-Pie". The only restrictions placed upon the World Citizen are those which he allows to contain him. Free is he to travel anywhere on the globe; the world as his wondrous playground.

The RPB is a citizen of the world. Armed with his human rights and his passport, the RPB/World Citizen navigates with the vision of a pioneer on the vastest of horizons. This is not some grandiose vision or fantasy, but a reality experienced by many today, right at this very moment...

The author has a challenge for anyone that is prepared to venture into the world of the World Citizen:

"I dare you to buy a passport. Even further I dare you to use it, anywhere, for anything. Feel the power you wield with it in your possession knowing that the only thing stopping you from leaving this landmass is a plane ticket or even gas money in some instances. Seize the day. He who hesitates is lost."

You must now familiarize yourself with a term that is known well to most international businessmen. This term is, *"expatriation,"* which is the process of becoming a national of a nation different from that of your birth. The expatriate citizen normally expatriates based on the business connection to the foreign nation. It is not uncommon for people to relocate to foreign lands and create businesses and become citizens of that land. Americans see this often, as foreign nationals come to the U. S. to start businesses and strive to obtain American citizenship. This option is protected by their *Human Rights*.

The *Universal Declaration of Human Rights,* was established by the United Nations in 1948. This document consists of 30 sections/articles or rights that are outlined, as universal rights of all humans. The RPB is well aware of his Human Rights and even travels with a copy of this document on his person for security against any wishing to violate any of these said rights. There are some articles of the Human Rights document that the RPB holds particularly close to his heart, and they are as follows:

Universal Declaration of Human Rights

Article 12

> *No one shall be subjected to arbitrary interference with his **privacy**, family, home or correspondence, nor to attacks upon his honour and reputation. Everyone has the right to the protection of the law against such interference or attacks.*

Article 13

1. ***Everyone has the right to freedom of movement*** *and residence within the borders of each state.*
2. ***Everyone has the right to leave any country, including their own, and to return to their country.***

Article 14

1. *Everyone has the right to seek and to **enjoy in other countries asylum from persecution**.*
2. *This **right may not be invoked** in the case of prosecutions genuinely arising from non-political crimes or from acts contrary to the purposes and principles of the United Nations.*

Article 15

1. ***Everyone has the right to a nationality.***
2. ***No one shall be arbitrarily deprived of his nationality nor denied the right to change his nationality.***

Just these few articles displayed here are enough to show why the RPB holds the Declaration of Human Rights in such high regard. These rights outline an almost cryptic message to the RPB to become a

World Citizen and break the restrictive chains of restrictive citizenship.

For those of you that question the patriotism behind such a notion as is suggested here, need only bear in mind that a surprising number of U. S. Senators have dual citizenship with Israel. If national leadership is in on the fun, anyone would be a fool to question whether the factor of patriotism is an issue here. Take the time out to enjoy life and all it has to offer you, without creating artificial restrictions.

In the world of media and politics there is a culture of propaganda and spin that resembles mind control more so than actual information or policy factors. Once the economy began to collapse there was a new culprit identified and demonized, and all but deemed criminal, in the court of popular opinion [media/politics]. What was the attribute of this dastardly entity that has sucked the blood out of the world's economy? This evil villain is called the Multinational Corporation (MNC). The MNC has been used as a political punching bag, and smeared across the media like these entities were destined to be "brought to justice". The actual crime committed only alluded to, but never claimed, and the culprit to be "charged" never firmly identified. What is a Multinational Corporation and why are they demonized, and yet apparently so untouchable? Let's take a closer look:

Multinational Corporation – *A corporation that has its facilities and assets in at least one country other than that of its origin. These companies normally have factories and offices in different countries and operate from a centralized headquarters where global management is conducted.* ***Very large MNC's have budgets that exceed those of many small nations***.

Nearly all multinationals have the habit of being American, Western European, and Japanese, including: BMW, Honda, Toshiba, Wal-Mart, Coca-Cola, AOL, and Nike. Those advocating multinational entities point out that they create jobs/wealth, and improve technology in countries lacking in such development. Those that oppose multinationals claim they have "undue political influence over governments", and can "exploit" developing nations as well as create job losses in their home nations.

The above insider definition and explanation is very telling as to what a multinational is and what type of power it possesses. Also called transnational corporations, multinationals used to go by a different title, that the author feels is no longer used by media and politicians, for fear of an increase in awareness, as to how these structures work. The former name used to describe these entities was Offshore Companies/Corporations (OC's). These companies are commonly referred to by international entrepreneurs as International Business Company (IBC), the are also called non-resident companies. There are a number of factors that prompt a business owner to establish an IBC, and these are, privacy, tax savings—or no taxes, and reduced start-up capital requirements offered by foreign nations.

There are a number of nations that have passed legislature that would appeal to international entrepreneurs—by offering tax benefits, and enacting privacy laws.

This is done by nations and jurisdictions intentionally to attract IBC activity in their countries. These companies know that there is an opportunity that is offered by these jurisdictions to help strengthen the economy of their countries.

The International Monetary Fund (IMF) refers to the countries that participate in the encouragement of IBC activity "Offshore Financial Centers," and identify these nations/jurisdictions in a "Background Paper".

The more noteworthy among these locations are:

- Hong Kong

- New Zealand

- Isle of Man

- Cyprus

- Dubai

- Bahamas

- Jersey

- Belize

- Panama

IBC's are governed by the nations that they are incorporated in and not the nations that they conduct business and banking affairs in. This is the ultimate "key" as well as the inherent "evil" that is attributed to the Multinational Corporation.

Politicians have used the issue of the MNC in areas that have been affected by job loss, and companies moving overseas. It is personally realized by the author, the devastation that can occur when an area is ravaged by the removal of jobs and the relocation of companies to foreign locations, but seeing that the author has no intentions of ever becoming a political or media figure, the issue of creating

corporations in any country so desirable
—even bringing factories and call centers
to the 'States'–sounds quite splendid
indeed. It is time for the 'common man'
to get his piece of the international pie, it
would seem.

While the term '*Multinational
Corporation*' is used to make this
structure sound unpatriotic or even
traitorous, the fact is, the opportunity
for dynamic and astronomical growth
and wealth creation is available to any
man who wishes to obtain it;
furthermore, anyone who would stand in
the way of a man's pursuit of happiness,
brings their own patriotism into question.
The companies seen as evil are seen as

such because they created legacies on the backs of hard-working Americans, and once commercial income tax was increased, they packed up and relocated their operations to countries that had "cheap labor" and low or no taxes imposed on IBC's. This sudden and abrupt action performed almost in concert by a host of companies caused a devastation in the U. S. economy, particularly in the Midwest. The RPB has no reason to worry himself with issues that concern the old regime, or consequences of offenses committed by others. Remember that the elimination of Falsehoods is one of the three primary objectives outlined in Chapter 2. Do not fall victim to lies and propaganda.

In some nations companies are referred to as *'legal persons'*. This is an obvious indication as to the secret philosophy encoded and interwoven within this text. The fact that these *'people'* do not have a *body* means nothing—*that is where you come in*—they can still be sued, paid, and *own property* just like any sentient *physical 'person'*. The fact that you can *create* as many 'persons' as you can *conceive* in your mind, will *birth* the revelation of *being able* to *exist without* a *social security number*. In other words, it is no coincidence that you are able to enter a *social security number or* an *employer identification number* in the same field... Stop and think about what is being implied here, for those wanting privacy above all from this text. Some things are not given as blatantly and delivered less straightforward—for good reason. For those that are able to see, bear witness, and for those that are able to hear, hearken unto the unspoken truth in the previous page. When operating and structuring Trusts is covered, in the next chapter, there will be more incite given as to the ability to become a virtual 'ghost in the machine'.

It is also noteworthy to mention that it is common for foreigners to assume names that are indigenous to the land they are expatriating to. The RPB considers this the *unwritten 31st Human Right*. The right to *change* ones *appellation...*

The rules of the World Citizen are defined by his creativity. While some may read this text and become inspired to go out and start a business or three, the true RPB will read and reread this text to decode its cryptic meaning and use this text as a Financial Flight Plan™ and *escape* route, when *troubled* times arise in the *world*.

One of the most important things to remember when seeking to maintain ones privacy and manage a large fortune, is to be content not portraying the role of the boss and merely and agent. You can delegate responsibility to others to act in behalf of your companies, or operate as a low level agent/trustee for the entities.

CHAPTER

5

Helping Hand

In some countries Nonprofit Organizations (NPO's) are called Nongovernmental Organizations (NGO's). This is a strong indicator of the power such an entity is capable of possessing, if properly placed and structured. While the multinationals are demonized the NGO is deified by the communities and nations serviced by the entity. They are given the keys to the cities and able to affect change on an economic, social, as well as a political scale. The RPB is a humanitarian first and a capitalist by design, so it is only fitting to participate in the lucrative universe that is the "not-for-profit" sector — while assisting the global community.

An NGO is a 'legal person' created with the intentions of launching humanitarian and/or charitable efforts; securing profits is not the primary objective. These organizations enjoy immunity from income taxes and are eligible for benefits/grants from government agencies. The Private Multinational NGO is the secret weapon of the RPB. With the exception of the Trust structure, there has never been a more comfortable entity structure to seek safe haven within than an NGO/NPO.

If one seeks to find the power of the nongovernmental organization, one need look no further than the grandest example of the NGO... The Church! The modern day Church is actually classified as religious organization and is actually designated under the NPO code (in the U. S.), making the "Church" a 'legal person,' thus surrendering its sovereignty under God to the state. The state determines whether the Church stays open and all of the prayers in the world can not reverse the decision of the state to close down the Church, if it wills. What's wrong with this picture?

In times past the Church was a powerful entity that governed and ruled the masses. It is through the faith and belief systems that the law was passed down and ultimately enforced. Cannon Law, established by the Catholic Church is a comprehensive government structure that outlines the law in every nation where the Catholic Church is established. The interesting factor about Cannon Law, is that it also includes crime and punishment [law enforcement] protocols. This gives a whole new meaning to "answering to a higher law". It was the domination of the Church that caused the colonists to flee to the Americas, for freedom to worship as they sought fit. This is just a mere example of the power that an NGO can have. It would seem, that when an organization opts to interest itself with things other than profits the array of interests that the entity can involve itself in is boundless. There is a small nation out there waiting for its technological, educational, and economic revolution, and the visionary that is capable of providing the vision for that nation, will have the ear of both the banker and the politician alike. Be creative in your endeavors, there is much to be gained in enlightening of a mass of people.

The RPB creates a cluster of NGO's that are not apparently connected to each other, or any other corporate entities previously created, these entities will also function as Beneficiaries. It all boils down to Trusts.

The Trust is a legal structure, that is based on a relationship whereby a person's (Grantor/Settlor) assets and property is managed by another *'person'* (Trustee) for the benefit of a third party (Beneficiary). The Settlor, which can be a 'legal person,' places assets and proper in the care of a the Trustee, who is to manage the assets, and issue the assets or property to the Beneficiary in the time specified, in the Deed of Trust (document that establishes a Trust). Trusts are generally created for estate planning and asset protection. There are various types of structures and the RPB carefully evaluates Trust laws to determine what structures best suit the agenda of the RPB.

Trusts can be revocable (reversible) or irrevocable (irreversible) in nature. In estate planning the typical types of trusts are Living Trusts (also called inter-vivos trust), which comes into affect during the life of the Settlor; and Testamentary Trusts, which only become effective after the death of the Settlor. There is also the Charitable Trust, which is established with the intention of contributing to the charity of the Settlor's choice, and often times, the Trustee's selection. This is one of the Trust structures that the RPB has a particular interest in, for he knows that he can use this structure in a myriad of ways, for protection and secrecy. The RPB realizes that it is just as good to control great wealth, than it is to 'own' it in ones own name. The over-inflated ego and desire for the spotlight are enemies of the RPB, who is content living the 'good life' without the scrutiny that comes with being a public figure. The Trust is the *'machine'* you will seek asylum within.

Just as there are jurisdictions classified as 'offshore' based on the laws they enact that are beneficial to the IBC, there are also countries that are best suited for creation of International Trusts. When looking to establish a Foreign Trust, the RPB must seek *new zeal* in a *land* that has provided privacy laws for Trusts that keep beneficiaries secret and respect the right of a Trust to not disclose its details or Deed of Trust to the government.

Discretionary Trusts allow the Trustee to have more decision-making ability, as to the Beneficiaries to the Trust. The discretionary element is added to the Trust that is to have various Beneficiaries that are undetermined. Purpose Trusts are trusts that have no Beneficiary, but rather are established for a specific non-charitable purpose (Charitable Trusts are technically considered Purpose Trusts, but never referred to as such). When looking to establish a Trust not intended for the filtration of for-profit funds (from corporations owned) to the non-profit entities controlled, the International Purpose Trust is ideal. If you are not clear what country to establish your Foreign Trust in, the encoded clue already given in this chapter must be deciphered.

Private Trust Companies (PTC's) are 'legal persons' established to operate as Trustees for the Trust. PTC's are used particularly in situations where the jurisdiction of the Trust's creation requires for a Trustee of a Trust be a 'resident' of that jurisdiction. The PTC will have no actual assets so a 'nil' tax return may be filed for the PTC. The PTC is established by a charitable *Decoy Trust*™, solely to incorporate and own the PTC. The only assets of the Decoy Trust will me the PTC shares owned (which have no value). This allows the RPB to control all entities without needing to appear to "own" anything at all. When opening bank accounts a limited Power-of-Attorney for the RPB or a relative or loved one to act as the account signatory/fiduciary agent is all that is needed to complete the smoke screen of privacy protection. Various layers of protection are added by creating more levels of PTC's and Decoy Trusts™. The creative RPB takes this model and customizes it as needed.

The following scenario will illustrate how the method may be executed by the RPB. There are three different nations/jurisdictions used in this example (A,B, and C). The scenario is as follows:

> The RPB creates a Decoy Trust in the in Country A (Business Country). This Decoy is used to establish a PTC in Country B (Trust Country). The PTC is used as the Trustee for the second Charitable Trust established to filter the funds from the for profits. (The for profits are created by a Private Trust that is established for the sole purpose of creating the for profits companies in Country A—

eliminating the connection to the RPB.)

Once the Charitable Trust in Country B is established, the RPB establishes a bank account for the Charitable Trust that will be filtering the for profit funds, in Country C (Banking Country). The separation of the elements of the Trust (Settlor, Trustee, and Banking) makes it more than difficult for anyone to determine who is actually in control. This same scenario can be duplicated to create various levels of protection by creating a series of PTC's and Decoy Trusts to shadow the origin, or mastermind behind the vast network of activity. The key is to maintain creativity and create degrees of separation between each entity, while also establishing a multinational network that will give any wannabe 'spy' a headache trying to unravel the origins of the RPB's clandestine empire. This will be nearly impossible to trace due to the *"floater's clause"* placed into the Deed of Trust that calls for the transfer of all Trust documents to a foreign jurisdiction at the first sign of prying eyes.

The above scenario is just a simple and quite humble example of the types of strategies the RPB will employ to keep his privacy while being able to control vast amounts of wealth globally. By banking in a different nation than the Trust Country, and also the Business Country, the funds are always out of reach of the curious.

The concepts described here relating to Trusts are very complex and known by only a few. The brief description given here is merely and overview and far from an absolute on establishing and operating Trusts. It is advisable that an attorney specializing in International Business Law is sought, to navigate across this demanding terrain, if needed. Offshore Attorneys seem to have a good grasp on many of the topics described here. All concepts that are new, will be easily grasped by any attorney gifted enough to decipher the road map laid out here.

It is a must that you become familiar with the term "Nominee Director". Nominee Directors make it possible to formulate companies and organizations in countries that require that a number of directors on the board of directors be residents of the nation of establishment. Nominee Directors possess no actual executive power and are merely used as 'stand-ins' or 'straw men'. These may also be 'legal persons'. The Nominee Director is not normally required to hold any shares/interest in the entity. An agreement is drafted to solidify the position as one of non-executive status.

In the modern era of the internet and text translators online (converts text to and from various languages), it is possible to locate nominees on foreign chat rooms and forums, and discuss these things in the native tongue of the nominee. The use of the Nominee Director is a trade secret of the RPB.

It is also important to mention that it is not uncommon for nations to hold their assets in Foreign Trusts. It should be apparent to you by now that the laws of commerce known no boundaries and have no loyalty to any state. In fact it is safe to say, that all countries operating under the code of capitalism have increased their wealth by making advancements in their "Foreign Policy" procedures. The far-reaching hand of commerce is the hand in which the RPB endorses the negotiable instrument that secures his eminent and luxurious future.

Birthing of Financial Institutions is another great power that the more sophisticated Trust structures possess. The concept of creating a virtually unregulated foreign Financial Institution will be explored later in this text. In conjunction with the NGO and Trusts, these institutions create the power that defines the RPB.

CHAPTER

6

Power to the People

A surprising number of areas have been virtually left for dead, and cut-off from the advancements and quality of living enjoyed by the 'developed' countries. Many countries deemed 3rd World, are in that position by design, and not merely by circumstance. The possession and application of appropriate knowledge is enough to catapult even the most desolate of countries to a technological revolution in the span of a decade. What is the primary element needed for a Technological Revolution? Why electricity of course!

The primary key to all technology is 'power'. However, it takes a certain degree of development to facilitate the production and distribution of power. When you hear of countries developing into capitalist countries, the first thing they mention is the word *'infrastructure'*. Infrastructure includes the physical and operational structures and implementations needed to empower an economy. Infrastructure includes roads, bridges, sewers, water-processing plants, power grids, and telecommunication installations, which enable the production of power; which allows for the production of factories and other businesses, which empower an economy, which creates consumers, who will in turn use their new found riches to benefit from the aspects of the 'Technological Revolution' they wish to participate in.

Technological advancement to a nation that is completely lost, as to the current trends of technology can be as simple as telephone and pager networks. Obsolete and out dated elements of our society far passed away can be astonishing wonders to a nation that has never known such treasures. The author would often in his youth think of what an ancient uncivilized people would think if a man appeared and possessed something as simple as a cigarette lighter. He would no doubt be at first feared by all; this fear would develop into intrigue by some, and eventually even develop into an almost deification or demonizing of that individual. This interpretation would differ based on what it was that party used the lighter for. He could choose to burn the village or help the people by building a fire. The RPB is not the arson, but rather the aider in the mission to bring light anywhere darkness exists.

It is not being suggested that the RPB fund the infrastructure of these nations, but rather influence the policy makers and provide a definitive plan that will not only assure re-election, but also an opportunity to monetarily gain from the developments to society. It is customary for corporations to produce much of the legislation that is passed. This is why lobbyist are so influential on *'capital'* hill. The corporate money is intricately woven in to the fabric of the political culture of the world. If you have not realized by now, being an RPB is not about reinventing the wheel, but rather about the inflation and the shining of the wheel, before it is placed on the wheelbarrow that the RPB pushes to the bank for his many massive deposits.

The RPB may contribute to the aspects of the infrastructure development that will benefit his cause. This may include water processing facilities and the formation of the power grid. The privatization of these sectors is heavily encouraged by the RPB. If the RPB is able to gain control of the water and power supply, the development of the area will directly correlate with the economic growth experienced by this Financial Juggernaut™. This strategy will elevate the RPB to a new stature of affluence, unrealized by typical entrepreneurs and moguls.

The process of development is accelerated by the RPB who provides the chosen politicians with the outline for the legislation that will initiate the infrastructure projects. It is common for corporations to structure legislation and present the drafts to the government, who then vote the legislation into effect.

A healthy amount of political pressure is placed upon politicians at the initial encounter with the RPB, who would have already used his canvasing planning strategies to gather petitions in support of infrastructure and technology, from the constituents of the politician. Politicians always look towards re-election, and make every move with the intentions of creating an image of effectiveness that will hopefully lead to the renewal of the term, or even the establishment of a legacy—for the politician who has exhausted his tenure.

The RPB is a master at gathering individuals for his causes, by offering them something in return. This is often only the opportunity to have their voices heard. Behind every great 'movement' there is an invisible hand that materializes the 'bankroll' for such efforts. Possession of that invisible hand makes the RPB more powerful than the politician, who will eventually become pressured by the outcome of the RPB's manufactured 'movement'. This outcome being obviously the gatherings of groups of concerned and/or excited citizens. This will inspire the pols to conform to the agenda of the RPB.

CHAPTER

7

YOU vs. You

History possesses an abundance of epic battles, that will forever etch themselves in our minds. Man versus Nature, Man versus Man, and Man versus Machine are classic categories for these themes. The more unsung of histories great battles are ironically the ones we participate in ourselves, to this very day. What fast food restaurants do you patronize—if any? What department stores do you patronize? Do you prefer name-brand or off-brand products? What type of clothes do you buy, and from where do you purchase these garments?

The answers given to the previous questions determines what side you have aided in the battle defined by the battlefield that is commerce. There is always a battle in commerce whether we wish to acknowledge it or not, and where there is battle, there are winners and losers. This is obvious when you watch major companies "slug it out" on the prime time network commercial spots.

These competitions gave birth to terms like "leading brand," which is basically an underdog statement appealing to those that tend to root for the underdog. The reverse to this position would be the company that wants to keep reminding you that they are the original, which in the minds of many, means that this company's long-held position makes this company the only obvious choice. People often pick sides in these battles in the same fashion that they choose teams to support in sports rivalries. Some people naturally root for the champion and some naturally root for the underdog. Knowledge of this secret makes the RPB a promoter of the most spectacular of battles, that will surely not disappoint. These battles are played out in a fashion never before disclosed or implemented by any company anywhere.

In instances where there is no competition in a market, and one company controls the entire market, this is called what?... That's right, a monopoly. Monopolization is frowned upon, and in most capitalist societies, illegalized in one way or another. Governments seek to break up monopolies and force the solo giant to share the playing field with competitors to make it a battlefield. This normally leads to the market being controlled by a small group of three or more companies.

When a small group of companies controls a market it is called an "oligopoly". It is popular belief that people deserve to have a choice, and this is very true. If consumers are forced to purchase from one company, this tends to cause resentment to fester towards that company; for a part of that consumer feels dependent on the company. The RPB knows this, and uses this to his advantage.

When seeking to initiate a market in a developing country, the RPB must use great tact, to not appear as an overbearing force in a community. While, the political-style campaigning helps some with the image, it will not be enough to break the stigma of apparent monopolization in the area. To avoid scrutiny and attempted regulation of the dominant position in the market, the RPB uses the power of the oligopoly to further increase his success.

To the authors knowledge, the strategy outlined here is unique to the RPB and virtually unused to date. This strategy is called the *"YOU versus You"* strategy. Here is how it works:

> The RPB starts a new IBC and starts business in an untapped market. This company is designed to give the appearance of a 'major' company. This is done in the typical fashion—with a lot of propaganda, and flashy ads with bright colors, and the constant

presence in peoples everyday lives. The study and duplication of the efforts of dominant companies that the RPB sees have etched out a legacy of success, provides the blueprint that he models his campaign after.

Once the market has been established and begins to flourish, the RPB switches gears, and does the unthinkable. He creates another IBC from a company not connected to the other company in any way—it may even be incorporated in a different nation than the first. The sole purpose of this company is to play the role of the underdog. This second company represents 'choice' to all that would like an alternative. This company will offer an inexpensive alternative to all that would like to benefit from the savings. This company intentionally does everything in a scaled down, but not quite generic way, to entice thrifty consumers.

The fun begins when the second company begins an advertising campaign that takes not-so-subliminal jabs at the "leading brand". This will fuel a battle that will amass great wealth for the

RPB, while giving the public its choice, and a good battle to participate in, to boot.

As stated earlier, an oligopoly consists of a group of companies that control a market, rather than only two; however, the RPB does not seek to generate the third company, for when a battle is brewing there will at some point appear a third company to engage in the battle. If and when this occurs, the next phase of the strategy goes into effect.

The third company will more than likely come in to take the

position of the smaller company, sandwiching the second company in the middle, taking away some of its underdog appeal. If the third company comes in and has more resources and wants to assume the top position, the first company has the appeal of being the 'original'. In this scenario the new company comes in to take the underdog's position.

Once the emergence of the third company (real competition) has occurred, the battle between the first two companies heats up, to distract people from the new companies presence. The fever of the battle will create great interest in the general public who have stood by these companies since they started. During the throes of battle, the first company unexpectedly swallows the second company in a buyout and consolidates the wealth of both entities into one mega company. This takeover serves two purposes. The first purpose, is to cement the position of the first company at the top, and the second is to put the new company on shaky ground and make the future of the market seem uncertain to the third company.

Now that there are only two companies remaining in the market, the plan gets even more intricate, as the RPB creates yet another company that is unconnected to the previous companies, to assume the position of the underdog. This move will sandwich the competitor in the middle, and take their underdog positioning away. Like the last go around, the RPB will not engage the competitor—who is 'stuck' in the middle—but rather engaged only the companies that he creates and ignores the real competition no matter how much they try to bait the RPB. This will make the competitor appear to be no more than an inferior entity attempting to bully the major company and feed off of the stragglers that stray from the entity. Since the competitor is no longer in the bottom/underdog position, much of the potency of their claim has faded, and they will appear to be in the way in the minds of many. Once the public has all but rejected the competitor, the stage will be set for the attempted take over of the competitor's company. The RPB makes this move in the tradition of the 'mercy killing' and expresses that the intention is to allow the competitor to cut their losses and exit the market without totally losing out. This is not a disingenuous move, for the RPB does truly wish to offer the competitor a constellation prize for their efforts and participation in the battle. This will create a void that another company will someday attempt to fill. This will start the process over again.

If the competitor refuses the RPB's attempts to buy the company, the RPB will create yet another unconnected company that will create a four way oligopoly. The competition will begin between the two small companies that the RPB controls and between the major and the minor companies, as well. This provides a host of battles, none of which the competition is actively participating in. This will eventually lead to the competition becoming obscure.

As long as the market is dominated by the companies controlled by the RPB, there is no need to destroy the competition —if they wish to stay in the market.

The example given here is a method that

can be used for practically any market when selling any product, service, or establishment in the world. This strategy is used by the RPB to establish a strong presence in a multitude of industrial sectors.

Once a market has fully been established, the RPB will serendipitously introduce regulatory NGO's into the picture. These entities will appear to surface as *'police'* over the market, and fabricate *'codes-of-law'* to be adhered to by the participants in the market. This will stop any attempts from the officials to regulate the RPB's entities. This solidifies the RPB's position and creates yet more avenues of wealth, as a permanent fixture in society.

CHAPTER

8

Gold is Good

Always remember the RPB Golden Rule: *"He who owns the gold makes the rules."*

This statement is not a joke but rather a simple fact of life. What type of billionaire would control billions of dollars without possessing gold to back this amassed wealth? The answer is, no type of billionaire at all would generate this level of wealth without actually owning something of *'real value'*. If you are of the mentality that paper currency is actually *'real money'*, the author encourages you to learn more about what happened to the gold standard in the U. S. and why Fort Knox no longer houses the gold that used to 'back' the financial system in that country. The history of gold and silver certificates— the original monetary notes issued before Federal Reserve Notes—is also of interest during the basic training stages for the RPB. The ramifications of House Joint Resolution (HJR) 192, shows the RPB what happened to the constitutional forms of money; said to be *"gold and silver coinage"* in that countries founding document. The fact is, that FRN's and all other forms of world currency are actual debt instruments backed by debt only. Any so-called money in this current day —save gold, silver, and other precious metals like platinum—is essentially worthless, but the *de facto* acceptance of these instruments, by all, has lulled the global society to sleep on the issue. As the world slumbers, the RPB builds *his* Fort Knox and secures his future as the emperor of his own glorious empire, by accumulating *real wealth.*

Nearly every great civilization that was formed throughout history was done so with gold sharing the stage in its glory, and in most cases funding the whole movement. A life-long student of history and the success and failures of others in the past, the RPB is more than just an entrepreneur that is seeking his next million, but rather liken unto a king that knows the life of a kingdom is to be long-lasting, and not as fleeting as success often is in the world of business. The destruction of the kingdom on the king's watch is unacceptable, and leads to the demise of not only the king, but all of those that have trusted their lives to the mission of the kingdom. This, in the king's mind, is not an option, so he builds and secures the treasure that will support his kingdom, and allow it to flourish and grow.

Forever keeping anonymity as a mantra,

the RPB obtains his gold and other precious metals secretly and holds these treasures in trust—away from prying eyes. The emergence of the *Digital Gold Currency* (DGC) has marked global monetary revolution to allow the general public to discretely purchase large amounts of gold. The RPB uses his community of NGO's and Trusts to calmly and steadily secure bullion from the providers of DGC's.

Digital Gold Currency is a form of 'electronic money' that is based on the trading value of the gold. This works in the fashion of the original gold certificate that was made obsolete by FDR in 1933. There are firms on the internet that provide these currencies and the RPB is interested in the firm that has the presence of their gold confirmed, and is also financially regulated. The accounts are managed like typical bank accounts, and gold is delivered in three days after it is requested. One company in particular has all of these features and is located in an offshore location near the U. K. Due diligence is the key when looking into this world of the DGC. The author is not proposing holding large sums in the DGC accounts of these companies, but rather using these companies as gold vendors, who are willing to sell gold to their patrons without restraint from any source, looking to oversee the amount of gold allowed for its *citizens*.

As you should know by now, the limits of the RPB are defined only by his creativity. Using the NGO's and Trusts as a finely-tuned orchestra, the RPB has the ability to amass a great deal of wealth, quietly and lawfully. For a greater indication of the various ways these structures can be used, please revisit Chapter 5 of this text.

Only the ultra-wealthy take the type of interest in gold that the RPB does. Rather than owning gold as a sideline investment, the possession of gold is the ultimate goal of the RPB. There are many ways to secure gold in society, and the DGC route is not being promoted as the only means to do so. The existence of

DGC firms does however, make the mission of securing *real wealth* for the RPB early on in his journey feasible.

As the RPB becomes substantially and comfortably wealthy using the flight plan given in these pages, the energy (gold) will propel this emperor of great fortune to do more with this treasure. He will seek to build institutions of wealth that will provide a never-ending circuit of revenue for the RPB. This is a feat that we shall discover next!

CHAPTER

9

Be the Bank

What use is great wealth, if it is not put to good use? The RPB is always mindful of his fellow man, and is always aware of the need of funding in any society. The natural progression of the RPB into an international financier is inevitable, and in the wake of a technological and economic revolution in a developing economy; this progression is well-timed.

Lending institutions are needed to sustain economies through lending practices, which facilitate the possession of real estate and credit development, in a capitalist society.

As with all things, the RPB takes an unconventional approach to the development of his financial institutions. The IBC structure saves the identity and protects the RPB from the typical regulations associated with owning a bank. The structure of interest to the RPB is know as the *"Offshore Financial Company"* (OFC).

OFC's are companies that are established based on the IBC model, and that means that these companies are established in one country and do business in another country. If you were clever enough to decipher what country in which to establish your Foreign Trust in Chapter 5, than you already know what country is best to seek when incorporating the OFC. This same country allows financial companies to conduct banking anywhere else in the world, without regulation of the foreign jurisdiction where the bank is conducting business.

The first rule, of forming an OFC, is that the institution is not to have the word *"bank"* in the title, or in any of the advertising for the institution. The title may contain words like "Savings and Loan", "Lending", "Depository",

"Financial", and even "Bancorp" are currently acceptable for these companies. Make no mistake about these institutions, for they hold the same powers that any other banking institution does. OFC's may provide the following services:

- Credit Card and Debit services

- Checking/Savings accounts

- Lending

- Wire transferring services

- Financial guarantees/instruments

- Marketing of investments

- Cash/Fund management services

- Payment processing services

- Certificate of Deposit

The OFC is not limited to the services mentioned, and possesses the same authority and powers as any other "bank". The OFC's home jurisdiction does statutorily govern the OFC, but there are no banking regulations enforced in this offshore jurisdiction on OFC's. The OFC is not under the jurisdiction of the countries where business is conducted, so the RPB does not have to worry about privacy issues or governmental regulation by the country it is conducting business within.

The OFC gives the RPB the opportunity to provide the citizens of the community serviced, with programs that federally regulated banks are unable to. This makes it impossible for federally regulated banks to compete with the creative and diverse program offerings provided by the OFC. From mortgage programs to business financing the RPB is prepared to create a standard that others won't dare challenge —they can't afford to.

The various techniques outlined in this text, when used in conjunction with the OFC, will advance the RPB to the position that is more powerful than that of the best politician money can buy. Evaluation and study of the banking system and *"Modern Money Mechanics"* is paramount to establishing a successful OFC.

CHAPTER

10

Platinum Parachute

What about the exit strategy? The life of the RPB is fast-paced, and high-powered; so, what happens when he has had enough? Just as the life of the typical entrepreneur was not enough for the RPB, the retirement plan for the RPB is equally as extravagant. While entrepreneurs are satisfied with mansions and estates, secured by a couple of guards and a surveillance system, the RBP is satisfied only with owning islands, secured by a humble, yet thorough, army of militarily-trained specialists and troops. This force is in place to protect the RPB and secure the treasure that the RPB has amassed.

Having built a career on building businesses and infrastructure, the RPB has acquired every skill necessary to develop a small sovereign nation. The years spent building his financial empire, were only preparation for his ultimate goal; becoming the ruler of his own sovereign landmass. The invisible hand of the RPB has opened every door required to establish this kingdom. We will explore how the RPB establishes this kingdom.

The plan begins with the purchase of at least one island. The RPB finds that these purchases are much easier than most people think. The RPB may wish to have remote islands located in various regions throughout the world. This will give him the opportunity to be near jurisdictions where business is being conducted, without having to stay within the confines of that jurisdiction. The RPB can also choose to purchase islands specifically to build infrastructure and factories to export goods to various businesses that are controlled by the RPB internationally. It is no great feat to find individuals that would like to escape to an island paradise for work—the mere thought will sound like a dream come true to some. The

RPB is looking not only for factory workers but also business and technical-minded individuals to control the islands established for commerce. The commerce islands are to act like mini-jurisdictions that operate under the sovereignty of the state that is established by the RPB. These islands represent the pension plan for the RPB, who by now has probably cashed-in on most of his businesses, and is looking to live the remainder of his days catching up on years of lost rest and relaxation.

It is important to purchase a fleet of airplanes, jets, ships, yachts, submarines, and helicopters. These vehicles will aid the *force* in the protection of the RPB and his islands. Retired and discharged military personnel are employed and used as the top tier in the force's ranks. This will keep the island free from piracy and attempted infiltration. Forever concerned about loyalty, the RPB has groups watching each other to make sure that the first signs of dishonor are reported and handled according to protocol, and all negative influences are immediately deported back to their country of origin. This method of justice will allow the RPB to develop a society without the worry of a prison system or a criminal element festering within his society. The RPB does not need to play an active role in the governing of the islands, in fact the RPB only establishes the law in the beginning, and makes sure that all parties in the governmental structure take an oath to uphold those laws, and all of their subordinates are to do the same. There must be a zero tolerance policy for corruption, and everyone must know that their position can easily be filled if they fall short of their duties—performance decreases and arrogance increases when people feel the show can't go on without them. Always reiterate how privileged they are to have the opportunity to live in this paradise and have such authority in such a jurisdiction. The RPB always maintains a thankful and giving heart, and consistently offers gifts and rewards to his people.

The RPB only visits the commerce islands, making sure to never stay too long in these locations. The true domiciles for the RPB are located on private islands that are protected like a fortress, complete with underground vaults for much of the gold supply owned by the RPB. The troops protecting the gold must never know what they are protecting, and the transport and securing of the gold must be done discretely.

There should be more than one private island used as the *home* of the RPB, who makes sure to always operate with the element of surprise and never compromises his anonymity. He has become a Recession-Proof Billionaire™ and there is nothing that anyone can say or do about that, for it is far too late. Firstly, he [Trustee] is the only one that knows how massive the fortune is, and how it was generated; and quite frankly, he only appears to be working under orders from some unseen mastermind, who operates from the shadows.

Well my friend, our journey has come to an end. I pray this book will fuel a burning desire within you to incorporate the protocols set forth herein for your success; and while *your* journey has only just begun, I fear this is...

The End

www.ingramcontent.com/pod-product-compliance
Lightning Source LLC
Chambersburg PA
CBHW070042210526
45170CB00012B/572

* 9 7 8 0 5 5 7 8 8 0 3 6 2 *